Y0-EGI-571

Corn is planted in spring and grows tall in summer.

Reading Vocabulary Words

tassels
frozen
factories

High-Frequency Words

corn	watered
things	given
grown	ten
huge	again

Building Future Vocabulary

These vocabulary words do not appear in this text. They are provided to develop related oral vocabulary that first appears in future texts.

Words:	*transform*	*process*	*fraction*
Levels:	Library	Library	Library

Comprehension Strategy
Summarizing information

Fluency Skill
Pronouncing difficult words accurately

Phonics Skill
Developing and applying knowledge of consonant digraphs: *sh* (fre<u>sh</u>)

Reading-Writing Connection
Writing a journal entry

Home Connection
Send home one of the Flying Colors Take-Home books for children to share with their families.

Differentiated Instruction
Before reading the text, query children to discover their level of understanding of the comprehension strategy — Summarizing information. As you work together, provide additional support to children who show a beginning mastery of the strategy.

Focus on ELL

- Demonstrate saying /sh/. Explain that the /sh/ sound is made by putting your teeth together and blowing air out.

- Have children put their hand in front of their mouth as they say /sh/. Ask *Do you feel air coming out of your mouth?*

Using This Teaching Version

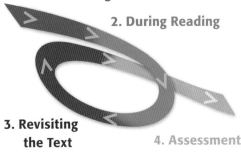

1. **Before Reading**

2. **During Reading**

3. **Revisiting the Text**

4. Assessment

This Teaching Version will assist you in directing children through the process of reading.

1. **Begin with Before Reading** to familiarize children with the book's content. Select the skills and strategies that meet the needs of your children.

2. **Next, go to During Reading** to help children become familiar with the text, and then to read individually on their own.

3. **Then, go back to Revisiting the Text** and select those specific activities that meet children's needs.

4. Finally, finish with Assessment to confirm children are ready to move forward to the next text.

Title I
Chamberlain Elementary
428 N. 5th St.
Goshen, IN 46528

Building Background

- Write the word *frozen* on the board. Read it aloud. Ask *What does it mean if something is frozen?* Ask children to name frozen things.

- Introduce the book by reading the title, talking about the cover photograph, and sharing the overview.

Building Future Vocabulary

Use Interactive Modeling Card: New Word Log

- Introduce children to the word *process*. Discuss its meaning as a series of steps leading to an end result or a finished product. Enter *process* and its meaning on the New Word Log. Repeat with the words *transform* and *fraction*.

- After reading, use the third column to record reasons this word is good for describing the book.

- Brainstorm other words that end with /sh/. Then brainstorm words that begin with /sh/.

Introduction to Reading Vocabulary

- On blank cards write: *tassels*, *frozen*, and *factories*. Read them aloud. Tell children these words will appear in the text of *Corn*.

- Use each word in a sentence for understanding.

Introduction to Comprehension Strategy

- Explain that when we summarize, we say in a few words what our reading is about. Say *Saying what the book is about helps you understand and remember what you read.*

- Tell children that they will be saying in their own words what they learn in *Corn.*

Introduction to Phonics

- Write **fresh** on the board. Read the word aloud, emphasizing the final /sh/. Write the *sh* digraph on the board and explain that the letters *s* and *h* have the sound /sh/.

- Have children practice saying /sh/ and **fresh**.

- Brainstorm other words that end with /sh/. Then brainstorm words that begin with /sh/.

Modeling Fluency

- Read the text on page 5 aloud. Point to *fresh* and say *Now we know this word, and we have practiced it.*

- Point out another potentially difficult word, *Mexico*, and repeat it slowly. Have children practice saying *Mexico.* Say *Now we have practiced the difficult words on this page, and we can read the sentences without stopping to think about these words.*

2 During Reading

Book Talk

Beginning on page T4, use the During Reading notes on the left-hand side to engage children in a book talk. On page 24, follow with Individual Reading.

During Reading

Book Talk

- **Comprehension Strategy**
  Ask *What is this book about?*
  (corn) Point out that the title
  Corn is a summary of the
  whole book in one word.

- Explain that the table of
  contents is a summary, too.
  The name of each chapter
  summarizes what the chapter
  is about. Ask *What is Chapter
  5 about?* (planting the seeds)
  What is Chapter 8 about?
  (harvesting the corn)

- Ask *Does one of these chapters
  sound interesting to you? What
  do you think that chapter is
  about?*

Turn to page 2 – Book Talk

Corn

Heather Hammonds

Corn

Heather Hammonds

Future Vocabulary

- Remind children of the meaning of the word *process* discussed earlier in the lesson. Explain that reading a nonfiction book is a *process* that begins with looking at the cover illustration or photograph, the title and author's name, and the table of contents.

- Say *Looking at the table of contents is a good way to get ready to read a book.*

Now revisit pages 2–3

During Reading

Book Talk

- Invite children to respond to the opening question of the book. Ask *Do you like to eat corn? What kind of corn do you like to eat?* (corn on the cob, popcorn, creamed corn, cornbread)

- Together look at the diagram of an ear of corn. Talk about the four parts that are labeled and about how the arrows and labels help us understand the diagram.

- **Comprehension Strategy** After reading page 3, model summarizing information. Say *This page is about ways people use corn. How do you use corn at your house?*

Turn to page 4 — Book Talk

Chapter **1**   **Corn**

Do you like to eat corn?
Corn grows on tall corn plants.
Corn plants are grown in many places around the world.

2

Corn is found in many different foods we eat.
Corn is made into animal food, too.

Corn is also made into other things.

silk

cob

kernels

fuel

husk

3

Future Vocabulary
- Ask *What are the tall plants in the photograph? What is the boy eating?* Explain that corn is transformed, or changed, from these forms to many other things, like the fuel in the can on page 3.
- Ask children if they have played with a kind of toy robot that can be transformed into something else, such as a car, an airplane, or an animal.

Now revisit pages 4–5

3

During Reading

Book Talk

- Ask children if they have seen corn growing. Ask them to tell where they saw the corn, what time of year it was, and what the corn plants looked like.

- **Phonics Skill** Have children find the word with the consonant digraph *sh* on page 5. *(fresh)* Have them read it aloud together, emphasizing the /sh/.

- **Comprehension Strategy** Model summarizing information. Point out that this chapter is about how corn was first grown thousands of years ago in Mexico and then taken to the rest of the world.

Turn to page 6 – Book Talk

Chapter 2

Corn Story

Corn plants are a kind of grass.
They grow in summer
when the weather is warm and sunny.

People have been growing corn plants
for thousands of years.

4

Corn was first grown in Mexico. People ate fresh corn and made flour from corn seeds.

Soon people from other countries began to grow corn, too.

Corn is also called maize.

5

Future Vocabulary

- Ask *What does the woman have to do to the corn seeds before she can use them to make the bread?* (pound or grind the corn seeds into flour) Explain that grinding the corn seeds into flour is the first step in the process of making the bread.

- Think out loud with children about other steps in the process: adding liquid to make dough, shaping the bread, heating the stone, baking the bread.

Now revisit pages 6–7

During Reading

Book Talk
- Ask *What are some foods that are made from ground corn flour?* (tortillas, cornbread) Ask children to think of other foods they have eaten that are made with corn, such as grits, polenta, cornflakes, corn chips, or tamales. Ask *Do you fix popcorn at your home? Where else do you eat popcorn?*

- **Comprehension Strategy**
  Model summarizing information. Ask *What is this chapter about?* (kinds of corn) *This chapter is about how different kinds of corn plants grow different kinds of corn and different colors of corn, too.*

Turn to page 8 — Book Talk

Chapter 3

Kinds of Corn

There are many different kinds of corn plants.

Some plants grow corn that makes good flour.

Some plants grow sweet corn that is good to eat.

corn flour

6

Some plants grow corn that is made into food for people and animals.

Some plants grow corn that makes good popcorn!

chicken feed

popcorn

Corn can be yellow.
It can be other colors, too.

7

Future Vocabulary

- Point out that the rectangle at the bottom of page 7 is divided into equal parts. Ask *How many equal parts are there?* (four) *Each part shows a different color of corn. What colors do you see?* (white, mixed white and yellow, yellow, mixed red and blue)

- Reproduce the rectangle and the four equal parts on chart paper. Explain that each part of the rectangle can be represented by a fraction. Write the fraction 1/4 in each of the four parts. Say *Each part is one fourth, or a quarter, of the whole. Where else do we use fractions?*

Now revisit pages 8–9

During Reading

Book Talk

- Ask *What does it mean to till the soil?* Explain that words in boldfaced type are in the glossary. Look up *till* in the glossary. Ask *What does it mean to harvest the crop?* Look up *harvest* in the glossary.

- Point to each of the photographs on page 8 and ask *What is the farmer doing?* (tilling, planting, harvesting) Ask children to point to the machines on these pages.

- **Comprehension Strategy**
  Model summarizing information. Ask *What is this chapter about?* (corn farms) *Farmers till, plant, and harvest on small corn farms and huge corn farms. If you were a farmer, would you rather have a small farm or a big farm? Why?*

Turn to page 10 — Book Talk

Chapter 4 **Corn Farms**

Most corn is grown on farms.

Some corn is grown on small farms. Farmers:

till the soil

plant the corn seeds

harvest the corn

8

Some corn is grown on huge farms.

Farmers use big machines to:
till the soil

plant the corn seeds   harvest the corn

Future Vocabulary

- Say *These pages are about three important steps in the process of growing corn.* Ask children to name the three steps. (tilling, planting, harvesting)

- Talk about how the process is different on a small farm and a big farm. Ask *How does the farmer on page 8 till the soil?* (with a digging stick) *How does the farmer on a big farm till the soil?* (with a machine) Ask children to contrast planting and harvesting in the same way.

Now revisit pages 10–11

During Reading

Book Talk

- Ask *What is a sprinkler?* Point out that *sprinklers* is in bold-faced type. Look up *sprinklers* in the glossary.

- Ask *What is the machine in the photograph on page 10 doing?* (tilling the soil) *What is the machine on page 11 doing?* (planting corn seeds)

- **Comprehension Strategy**
  Model summarizing information. Ask *What is this chapter about?* (planting the seeds) *This chapter tells how the farmer tills and waters the fields and then puts the seeds, plant food, and weed and insect killers into the soil.*

Turn to page 12 — Book Talk

Chapter 5 **Planting the Seeds**

It is spring at this big corn farm.
It is time to plant the corn seeds.

The corn fields are tilled.

They are watered with big **sprinklers**.

tilling the corn fields

10

The corn seeds are planted in long rows.
Plant food is put into the soil at the same time.

Sometimes weed and insect killers
are put into the soil, too.

11

Future Vocabulary

• Say *This chapter is about planting the corn. We learn more about this step in the process. What things are put into the soil during the planting?* (water, seeds, plant food, weed and insect killers)

Now revisit pages 12–13

Book Talk

- Ask *How long does it take the corn plants to grow out of the soil after the seeds are planted?* (seven to ten days) Ask children to point to the photograph that shows the corn plants when they first come out of the soil. Ask *How tall do the corn plants get?* (taller than the farmer)

- **Comprehension Strategy** Discuss the list of corn plant requirements on page 13 and how it is a summary of information, too. Ask *What things do people need to live?* Use children's suggestions to make a list similar to the one on page 13. Compare and contrast the needs of corn plants with the needs of people.

Turn to page 14 — Book Talk

Chapter 6 **Growing Tall**

The corn plants grow out of the soil seven to ten days after the seeds are planted.

The plants are watered again as they grow. They are given more plant food, too.

12

Revisiting the Text

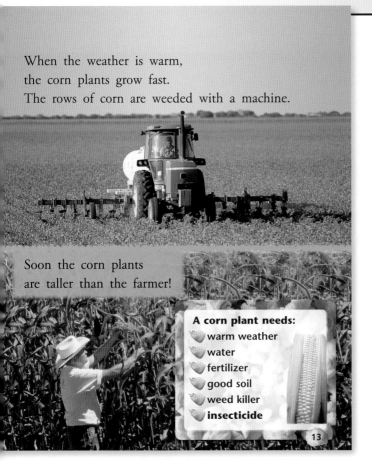

When the weather is warm,
the corn plants grow fast.
The rows of corn are weeded with a machine.

Soon the corn plants
are taller than the farmer!

A corn plant needs:
- warm weather
- water
- fertilizer
- good soil
- weed killer
- **insecticide**

13

Future Vocabulary

- Say *Let's read aloud the list of things that are needed to transform a corn seed into a tall corn plant.* Have individual children read items from the list on page 13.

Now revisit pages 14–15

During Reading

Book Talk

- Point out that five words on these pages are included in the glossary. Look up the words.

- Hold up the word card for *tassels*. Say the word aloud and have children practice saying it with you and individually. Show children a textile *tassel* or a picture of a *tassel* on a pillow or ski cap.

- **Comprehension Strategy** Model summarizing information. Say *These pages are about how pollen from* tassels *falls on the silks and the corn begins to grow inside the ears.*

➜ *Turn to page 16 — Book Talk*

Chapter 7 **Tassels and Silks**

It is summer on the farm.

Tassels grow on top of the corn plants.

14

Little **ears** of corn grow on the stalks. Lots of thin **silks** grow from the ears of corn.

silks

Pollen from the tassels falls down onto the silks. Then the corn begins to grow inside the ears.

You can see lots of corn silks inside this **corncob**.

15

Future Vocabulary

- Look at page 14 and ask *What do you see in the photograph on the top half of the page?* (a big cornfield) *What do you see in the photograph on the bottom half of the page?* (cornstalks with tassels)

- On chart paper draw a rectangle representing the book page. Draw a line dividing the top half from the bottom half. Say *Half is another fraction.* Write 1/2 in each half of the rectangle.

Now revisit pages 16–17

During Reading

Book Talk

- Look at page 16. Ask *What do you think the man in the photograph is doing?* (looking at an ear of corn to see if it is ready to harvest) *How does the farmer know when the corn is ready to harvest?* (when there are lots of little kernels on each cob) Look at page 17. Ask *What is the machine in the top photograph doing?* (dropping harvested ears into a bin) *What is the machine in the bottom photograph doing?* (taking kernels off the corncobs)

- **Comprehension Strategy**
  Model summarizing information. Ask *What is this chapter about?* (harvesting the corn) *This chapter is about how the ears are harvested after about 70 to 100 days.*

Turn to page 18 – Book Talk

Chapter 8 Harvesting the Corn

The corn grows bigger and bigger.
Soon there are lots of little kernels on each cob.
It is time to harvest the corn.

It takes around 70 to 100 days
before corn is ready to harvest.

16

Big machines cut the corn plants
and take the ears of corn from the stalks.
The corn plants are left behind in the corn field.

Some harvesting machines
can also take the kernels
off the corncobs.

17

Future Vocabulary

- Say *The next step in the process is harvesting. When does the farmer harvest the corn?* (after 70 to 100 days, when there are lots of little kernels on each cob)

Now revisit pages 18–19

17

During Reading

Book Talk

- Ask *Have you seen corn that came in a can? Have you seen corn that came frozen in a plastic bag or a carton? Have you seen fresh corn on the cob that was still in its husk?* Have children share their experiences with various forms of corn.

- Hold up the word cards for *frozen* and *factories*. Say the words aloud and have children practice saying them with you and individually. Ask *What is a factory?* (a place where something is made) Together brainstorm things that are made at a factory.

Turn to page 20 – Book Talk

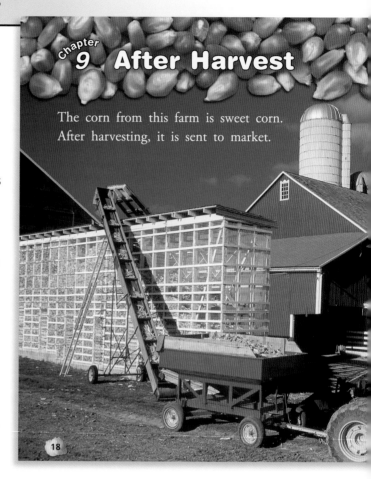

Chapter
9 After Harvest

The corn from this farm is sweet corn. After harvesting, it is sent to market.

18

Sweet corn can also be canned or frozen at factories.

Other kinds of corn are sent to factories and made into other things.

At some farms, cornstalks are harvested, too.

The cornstalks are used for animal food.

19

Future Vocabulary

- Ask *What happens to sweet corn after it is harvested?* (Some goes fresh to market, and some is canned or frozen.)

- Say *Canning and freezing are two ways to process vegetables so they will last a long time.* This is another way to use the word *process*.

Now revisit pages 20–21

19

During Reading

Book Talk

- **Comprehension Strategy**
  Model summarizing information. Say *This chapter is about what happens after the corn harvest is over. What happens at the farm after the corn is harvested?* (Cows eat the cornstalks; the fields are plowed; the farmer grows hay.) *When will the farmer plant corn seed again?* (next spring)

Turn to page 22 – Book Talk

Chapter **10 Back at the Farm**

After the corn harvest is over,
the farmer may let his cows eat the old cornstalks.
Then the fields are plowed again.

a field of old cornstalks

20

The farmer grows hay in the cornfields in autumn and winter.
More corn will be planted next spring!

Future Vocabulary

- Say *The harvest is over, and the cornfields have been transformed!* Have children review the transformation of the fields from planting through harvesting.

Now revisit pages 22–23

During Reading

Book Talk

- Leave this page spread for children to discover on their own when they read the book individually.

Turn to page 24 – Book Talk

Chapter 11 Grow Your Own Corn

You can grow your own corn.
You will need:
- warm weather
- a place to grow the corn
- plant food
- water
- corn seeds

22

Plant your corn seeds in rows,
just like farmers do.
Give them lots of water and plant food.
When the corn is ready, you can eat it!

23

Future Vocabulary

- Say *This chapter is about growing your own corn. Let's list the steps in the process.* (plant seeds in rows, add water and plant food, harvest)

- Say *This boy's corn crop is just a fraction of the farmer's corn crop.* Explain that sometimes the word *fraction* can mean "a small part."

*Go to page T5 —
Revisiting the Text*

During Reading

Book Talk
* Note: Point out this text feature page as a reference point for children's usage while reading independently.

Individual Reading

Have each child read the entire book at his or her own pace while remaining in the group.

**Go to page T5 –
Revisiting the Text**

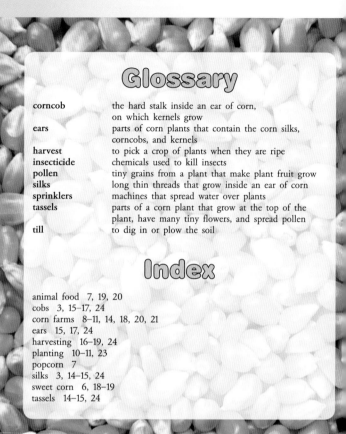

Glossary

corncob	the hard stalk inside an ear of corn, on which kernels grow
ears	parts of corn plants that contain the corn silks, corncobs, and kernels
harvest	to pick a crop of plants when they are ripe
insecticide	chemicals used to kill insects
pollen	tiny grains from a plant that make plant fruit grow
silks	long thin threads that grow inside an ear of corn
sprinklers	machines that spread water over plants
tassels	parts of a corn plant that grow at the top of the plant, have many tiny flowers, and spread pollen
till	to dig in or plow the soil

Index

24

During independent work time, children can read the online book at:
www.rigbyflyingcolors.com

Future Vocabulary

- Use the notes on the right-hand pages to develop oral vocabulary that goes beyond the text. These vocabulary words first appear in future texts. These words are: *transform*, *process*, and *fraction*.

Turn back to page 1

Reading Vocabulary Review
Activity Sheet: Sentence Maker

- Have children write *frozen* at the top of the Sentence Maker. Ask *What frozen things might be in a freezer at your home? What outdoor things are frozen when it is very cold?*

- Have children complete the Sentence Maker by writing three sentences using the word *frozen*.

Comprehension Strategy Review
Use Interactive Modeling Card: Summarizing Chart

- Use the Summarizing Chart to review the process of growing corn on a big farm.

- Model revisiting the book to review steps in the process. In the top three boxes, list information about planting, growing, and harvesting.

- Summarize the information in the bottom space.

Phonics Review

- Restate that the letters *s* and *h* have the sound /sh/.

- Reread page 5 and have children clap when they hear the word that ends with /sh/. *(fresh)*

Fluency Review

- Display page 19 and the word cards for *frozen* and *factories*. Have children practice saying the words. Have children find and practice reading other difficult words on the page.

- Partner children and have them take turns reading page 19. Ask children to help each other pronounce words accurately.

Reading-Writing Connection
Activity Sheet: Story Sequence Chart

To assist children with linking reading and writing:

- Have children complete the Story Sequence Chart by listing in order the things they would do if they grew their own corn.

- Have children pretend to be farmers and write a journal entry about a special day during the planting, growing, or harvesting of their corn.

4 Assessment

Assessing Future Vocabulary

Work with each child individually. Ask questions that elicit each child's understanding of the Future Vocabulary words. Note each child's responses:

- How is the world transformed after a snowstorm? In summer? In autumn?
- What are three steps in the process of making a peanut butter and jelly sandwich?
- Which of these is a fraction: 14 or 1/4?

Assessing Comprehension Strategy

Work with each child individually. Note each child's understanding of summarizing information:

- In one word, what is this book about?
- In your own words, how does a farmer grow corn?
- What is Chapter 2, "Corn Story," about?

Assessing Phonics

Work with each child individually. On chart paper write the words *ship, dash, shoe, show,* and *fish.* Have children underline the *sh* digraph if it is at the beginning of the word. Have them circle the *sh* if it is at the end. Have children read each word aloud. Note each child's responses for understanding consonant digraph *sh:*

- Did each child recognize the digraph *sh* at the beginning of words? At the end of words?
- Did each child understand that the *sh* digraph makes /sh/?

Assessing Fluency

Have each child read page 19 to you. Note each child's understanding of the pronunciation of difficult words:

- Was each child able to decode and accurately read the reading vocabulary words *frozen* and *factories*?
- Was each child able to read smoothly without slowdowns to pronounce other difficult words?

Interactive Modeling Cards

New Word Log

Title: *Corn*

New Word	Meaning in the Book	Why I Think the Author Chose the Word
process	list of steps	Corn goes through different steps.
transform	change	Corn and corn fields go through many changes.
fraction	part	Farms differ in size.

Directions: With children, fill in the New Word Log using the words *process*, *transform*, and *fraction*.

Summarizing Chart

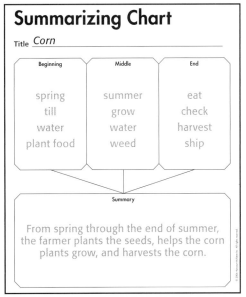

Title _Corn_

Beginning	Middle	End
spring	summer	eat
till	grow	check
water	water	harvest
plant food	weed	ship

Summary

From spring through the end of summer, the farmer plants the seeds, helps the corn plants grow, and harvests the corn.

Directions: With children, fill in the Summarizing Chart for *Corn*.

Discussion Questions

- Where was corn grown first? (Literal)
- Which comes first, tilling or weeding? Why? (Critical Thinking)
- Why does the farmer want to kill insects in the cornfield? (Inferential)

Activity Sheets

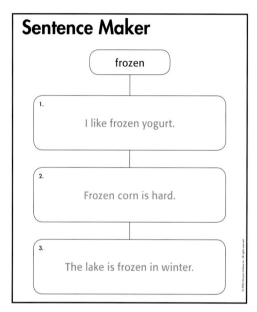

Sentence Maker

frozen

1.
I like frozen yogurt.

2.
Frozen corn is hard.

3.
The lake is frozen in winter.

Directions: Have children fill in the Sentence Maker using the word *frozen* in three sentences.

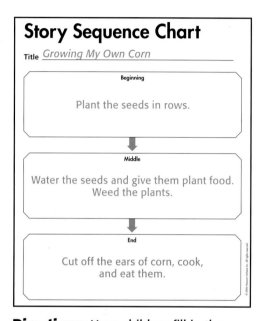

Story Sequence Chart

Title *Growing My Own Corn*

Beginning
Plant the seeds in rows.

Middle
Water the seeds and give them plant food. Weed the plants.

End
Cut off the ears of corn, cook, and eat them.

Directions: Have children fill in the Story Sequence Chart to explain how they can grow their own corn.
Optional: Have children write a journal entry about a special day during the cultivation process.